The Prospect Will Beg For A Solution!

ROBERT E. KRUMROY

Illustration and design by Jerry Odom

I-B Publishing, Greensboro, NC

ISBN 10: 0-9678661-7-0

ISBN 13: 978-0-9678661-7-8

Dedication

This book is dedicated to the many sales professionals and managers who selflessly give of themselves to help new agents; who share their knowledge and encourage them to persevere when times are tough, stick it out and build careers that will impact lives and add to the security of millions of families.

It is with great indebtedness and appreciation that I acknowledge my early year encouragers: David Sorensen, Vern Kuiper, and Larry Sterkenberg.

Thank you. You all changed my life ... and hopefully, I have changed others.

Preface

This book was written to help you maximize your selling capacity and to help you learn to communicate problems in a way that compels the prospect to ask for a solution.

By knowing the secret to attracting prospects (as identified in my previous books) and gaining the skill to sell the problem, you now have the combination that prepares you to hit the career homerun. Not just once, not by happenstance, and not because fate has finally blessed you with a good day—but because you can now attract prospects and sell problems in a way that works every time.

SELL THE PROBLEM. The prospect will BEG for a solution.

Contents

SECTION ONE

Foundational Principles for Achieving Super Sales Success

SECTION TWO

The Six Steps of Problem Communication

SECTION 1

Foundational Principles for Achieving Super Sales Success

CHAPTER 1
Sell the Problem

Super sales professionals *sell problems*, not solutions!

Recommendations are never implemented until the prospect determines that the cost of the problem is more painful than the cost of the solution.

When the prospect buys the pain, the loss, the unwanted consequences of the problem, nothing else matters—not even the cost of the solution.

Are you beginning to think about a sales attempt that failed because your solution was presented to the prospect before the problem was adequately sold?

Sell the problem, if you want to be an all-star in sales.

CHAPTER 2

Learn the Skill of
Problem Communication

Great sales professionals know that most of their failed sales attempts happen not because they made a bad first impression or made a bad solution presentation. It's because they didn't make a good problem presentation.

Consider the last sale you missed or the opening interview that stopped prematurely. Was the explanation of the professional way in which you work inadequate? Did you make a bad product presentation? Was your explanation of features and benefits deficient?

Or ... did you fail to sell the pain, the loss and the unwanted consequences of the problem before engaging the prospect in a discussion about your solution, product or planning process?

I bet you know the answer.

CHAPTER 3

The Prospect Must Verbally Admit a Need

You don't have an engaged prospect until your prospect verbally admits to having a need.

Let me bring your attention to the word *verbally*.

Most advisors focus on identifying a general problem in the initial face-to-face interview so that they can legitimize the discussion of their solution or service. However ... if you don't get the prospect to emotionally feel the pain of the problem as it may personally affect him or her, see the loss, face the future of unwanted consequences due to inaction, and then verbally admit to having a need, you don't have a prospect — not one who is going to be actively and genuinely interested in listening to your presentation.

If you want to maximize your sales results,

you must engage the prospect in a two-way, intensified pain discussion in your initial engagement.

If you don't, most prospects will say no to your recommendation or to your request to continue the interview process.

A word of caution: Getting the prospect to simply agree that he or she has a problem is not the same as getting the prospect to verbally interact to having a problem after discussing the painful depth of the consequences if the problem is not addressed. It may sound the same, but it's not. The interaction is the main ingredient to getting more prospects to say yes to continuing the sales process and to eventually getting more, bigger and easier sales.

CHAPTER 4

Be a Sales Person *First...* versus a Solution Professional

When a consumer encounters a crisis-apparent need, such as hair loss due to cancer treatment or termite destruction in the walls of their home, you can present a solution without a thorough discussion of the pain and unwanted consequences of the problem. Why? Because the problem and the personal pain are apparent to both parties, which allows you to focus on being a solution professional.

Conversely, when you are in the financial services industry, to get a prospect to agree that he or she needs your product is dependent first on getting the prospect to emotionally feel the pain and realize the unwanted consequences of the current situation. Therefore ...

you must fix your attention first on being a sales person – selling the problem – with the second objective of being a solution professional.

The difference is much more than a play on words.

Problem communication is a six-step procedure. Each step moves the potential client closer to a sale.

Most failed sales attempts are due to prematurely moving the prospect to the next step before he or she is emotionally prepared.

Here are the six steps, followed by a recommended percentage of interview time you should spend on each step before moving to the next step.

Step 1. State the Problem (5%)

Step 2. Awfulize the Problem (70%)

Step 3. Invalidate Other Alternatives (5%)

Step 4. Make a Statement of Hope (5%)

Step 5. Summarize the Pain, Loss
     and Unwanted Consequences (10%)

Step 6. Request Specific Action
     with a Benefit Statement (5%)

SECTION 2

The Six Steps of
Problem Communication

CHAPTER 5

Step One:
State the Problem

This step should encompass 5% of your first meeting.

Make a general statement about the problem you believe the prospect is encountering and obtain a general agreement—which may be a simple "yes" as a response to an affirmation question. Many advisors often think the prospect's financial problem is so transparent that the prospect automatically sees the problem as clearly as they do. WRONG!

Not getting the prospect's acknowledgment of the problem before proceeding to the next step is a fatal mistake.

HERE IS THE "HOW-TO"

To establish the foundation of your conversation, make a clear two- or three-sentence statement explaining the problem you want to address. Remarks about your company, firm, product or process will not accomplish this vital step. This is a common mistake. Don't make it!

Once you make a clear problem statement, ask for a general agreement that it is an area of concern for the prospect.

EXAMPLE 1
General Financial Statement

"*Fortune Magazine* featured an article titled 'The Future of Retirement: It's Not What You Think.' The number of people who bought this issue of the magazine off the rack caught *Fortune Magazine* totally by surprise. But if you think about today's economic environment, I believe you will agree that most people feel that being financially secure at retirement is a more difficult objective than in years past. Would you agree?"

(Pause. Let your prospect answer the question.)

"That's the area in which I focus my work."

EXAMPLE 2
The Long-Term Care Statement

"Did you know that more than 50% of us will need long-term care during our retirement years and that the average cost will exceed $60,000 or $70,000 per year, depending on where you live? That's a lot of risk and a lot of money. If you were retired, how many years do you think you could pay that bill from your savings before having a serious financial setback?"

(Pause. Let your prospect answer the question.)

"That's an area in which I focus my work—helping couples avoid depleting their retirement assets or crippling a spouse's ability to survive when a large amount of their retirement income could be required to go toward long-term care for their loved one. Would you agree that long-term care costs are a potentially growing threat for many couples in America?"

(Pause. Let your prospect answer the question.)

IT'S YOUR TURN

Write a three- or four-sentence statement that describes the problem area where you focus the majority of your work. Make it compelling and emotional – as though you were presenting it to a prospect. Remember, this statement is not about you, your product or your company. It's about a potential financial problem that your prospect may face.

CHAPTER 6

Step Two:
"Awfulize" the Problem

This step should encompass 70% of your first meeting.

Think about a sale you attempted in which your effort failed. Did you make a bad product presentation or an inadequate problem presentation?

This step is often completely overlooked and almost always shortchanged. Yet no step in problem communication is more important or more effective in leading your prospect to action. Take your time and get the prospect involved in an interactive discussion about the problem. If you don't, your chances of getting a sale will be dramatically reduced.

Discuss the pain, loss and unwanted consequences that will occur if the problem is ignored. This is no time to be timid.

Take the prospect, and the problem, to the depths of despair, with a discussion of how it could affect him or her personally.

This is your greatest opportunity to move the prospect to take action.

The sale is made when the pain of the problem is sold — not the product.

The sale is lost when you don't sell the problem intensely enough.

After presenting the problem, ask how your prospect feels about the problem and how it may affect him or her *personally*. Ask the client to elaborate, in order to solidify an emotional buy-in to the problem.

If the prospect's answer is weak, you didn't do an adequate job of personally identifying the pain of the problem. Try again and initiate a two-way discussion. Don't move to another issue. Sell the problem now ... or it won't get sold later.

> **If the prospect doesn't buy the cost of the problem, he or she is not ready to buy the cost of your solution.**

HERE IS THE "HOW-TO"

I once had a home built on a slope overlooking the fourth green of a country club golf course. My backyard was landscaped around a large swimming pool. One morning when I awoke and looked out the back window, I noticed that the water in the pool appeared higher on one side than the other. Throwing on my bathrobe, I ran outside and within moments verified my fear. The backside of the concrete pool had sunk. It was two inches lower than the front side.

I quickly called a company called The Pool Doctor. Three hours later, an odd little man wearing a white smock with a stethoscope around his neck appeared at the front door. Directing him to the back of the house, I watched from the inside sunroom overlooking the pool. With no hesitation, he dropped to his knees, placed the stethoscope on the pool's concrete decking and began a slow crawl around the perimeter while listening as though searching for a heartbeat. After twenty minutes, with my level of anxiety finally outweighing my patience, I walked out to see if I could get his diagnosis.

"Well, what did you find?" I asked.

"It appears that you have a leak in your pool," was the response from the Pool Doctor.

"I assumed that was the case when I called you. Do you know where it is or how severe it is?" I queried.

"It is over here in the corner. It appears that the water loss is fairly steady," came his reply.

"What do you think we will need to do to correct it and how much do you estimate it will cost?" I asked.

"I will need to take the readings I got back to my office, look at the schematic of the pool and determine how to best remedy your situation before I can answer that," he said.

Impatiently I asked, "Well, don't you have an idea of cost? I mean is this closer to a $2,000 repair, a $12,000 repair or what? I am sure you have encountered this before. Can you at least give me an approximate guess?"

Being noticeably agitated, the little man came closer to me, grabbed the inside of my arm and turned me around to face the back of my house, while he uttered the following:

"Mr. Krumroy, I want you to look at your house. It is a beautiful home. I assume you have had a lot of memorable times at this pool. But I want you to take a look at the two sides of your house. I want you to notice that if we have to bring large equipment into the backyard to remove a collapsed pool, we will either need to remove your retaining wall from the ten-foot elevated driveway on the right, which is really impossible, or remove the two large 100-year-old oaks to the left, the brick wall that separates you from the neighbor, demolish the pool house and destroy the gazebo. The two structures alone will exceed $60,000 to rebuild, not to mention the landscaping and the sizeable cost to remove the pool.

Additionally, if you don't correct the problem, how much do you think it will cost to repair the fourth hole of the golf course when your collapsing pool washes it out? And once your pool collapses, how would you suggest that we remove the old concrete before installing a new pool?"

Now, getting firmer and more descriptive, he continued:

"If we have to remove this pool, let me tell you what we would need to do! We would need to bring in about fifteen men with jackhammers and wheelbarrows, because we can't get large equipment back here. Then we would jackhammer out sections — piece by piece by piece. It would be tedious, slow and costly, not to mention the disruption for weeks or months to your personal sanity. Once the old pool was removed, we would then need to somehow re-dig your pool foundation, walk iron bars and plywood from the street to the back of your house to form the pool walls and then pump concrete from the street to complete the build-out.

Mr. Krumroy ...

does this give you an idea of what it is going to cost if you don't fix the problem? That's the big issue!

If you don't fix this problem, the cost is going to be monstrous.

So ... if you will allow me to go back to my office and look at the issue in more detail, I will be back tomorrow with a plan to fix the leak and provide pricing that will alleviate the bigger cost you will incur if you *don't* fix the pool. Would it be okay with you if we proceeded in that fashion? If not, I will leave and wish you the best."

Wow!!! What a salesman!

The next day he arrived around 2 p.m. He asked if we could sit at the table and review his proposal. Barely getting to the table, I immediately asked that we skip the proposal and look at the last page. I didn't want the details. All I wanted to know was how much the repair would cost. When he responded that it was going to cost $14,000, my only question was ... *"When can you start?"*

The sale was made through "awfulizing" the potential destruction that the problem could cause.

It was made by having me visualize the extensiveness of the problem, rather than just telling me that we had a crack in the pool and then presenting the solution.

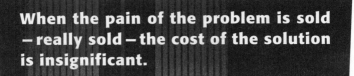

When the pain of the problem is sold – really sold – the cost of the solution is insignificant.

How many sales have you lost by not adequately selling the problem? When you don't involve the prospect in a two-way conversation about the cost of the problem, you will receive little interest back in implementing a solution.

EXAMPLE 1
Awfulizing Financial Issues

Understanding that the sale is made when the problem is sold, let's translate that from swimming pools to insurance and financial issues.

It is quite easy to find financial magazines with articles and front covers that accentuate the anxiety, difficulty and failure of many people in their quest to achieve the American Dream. Go to your local bookstore and find a magazine or article that illustrates this point (like the example below). A magazine has far more credibility than a company brochure. Here is the type of dialogue you should have with a prospect:

"Mr. Prospect, I am sure you have seen numerous articles in magazines like this one. The article attests to the difficulty and sometimes the failure of people to achieve their financial dreams.

As you can see, *Fortune Magazine* published this mid-year financial edition with a cover titled 'The Future of Retirement: It's Not What You Think.' The words, which overlaid the picture of a dock on a tranquil lake with two empty Adirondack chairs, made the message quite poignant. [Note: You may still be able to order a copy of this August 19, 1996, issue from *Fortune*.]

Candidly, I don't think that the photographer was holding back the throngs of people waiting to sit in those chairs while trying to get just the right lighting. I think he took the picture, walked off the dock and the seats were still unoccupied, which is rather symbolic of how fewer people are reaching their retirement dreams than at any time in recent history.

Let me mention that this issue of *Fortune* was one of the fastest-selling in the magazine's history. It went through numerous reprints to meet demand.

Now ... do you think *Fortune Magazine* is read by highly educated people or less-educated people? Do you think it is read by people who are more affluent or less affluent? It is read by highly educated, affluent people. So why do you think highly educated, affluent people bought this edition faster than most any other published issue? Because they know that retirement is becoming more difficult and that answers to the

When he responded that it was going to cost $14,000, my only question was... "When can you start?"

retirement dilemma seem more complex today than in years past.

This issue of *Fortune* was such a success that *Money Magazine* decided to put out an issue that it hoped would be as popular. The October 1996 edition of *Money* was titled 'Retire with All the Money You'll Ever Need.' On the cover was a photo of a couple with this caption: 'Bill and Barbara Bixler of Portland, Oregon, get everything they want out of life on 28% of their former income.' Everything they want on 28% of their previous income? You have got to be kidding. Well, here's what happened.

Bill Bixler, somewhere around 60 years old, was caught in a corporate downsizing and decided that he and his wife, Barbara, would just retire. After considering their options, he decided that he might need some professional advice. *Money Magazine* heard of his dilemma and stepped in with an offer to have financial professionals review their situation and offer advice for free, if they could use the couple in a feature article.

After careful fact-finding and consideration, the financial professionals selected by *Money* came up with the following recommendations.

First, they decided that Bill would need a part-time job to help meet his financial requirements.

Due to his age, they recommended he find a job that was not too strenuous.

Second, they recommended that he consider working at a movie theater. It wasn't strenuous; it would add the funds he needed for groceries; and, as a bonus, the theater would allow the Bixlers to watch movies for free. Wow! That was some in-depth professional advice. Wouldn't you agree? Yeh, right!

Third, they suggested that since the Bixlers were older and now retired, fashion was no longer a priority and Barbara could easily cut back on her wardrobe.

I am sure that when this report was finished, Bill and Barbara were glad they didn't have to pay for this professional advice.

My point is this: If you're like most people, someday you are going to retire with only three sources of income.

The first source is Social Security. Let's draw a small box, put the words 'Social Security' in it and put an arrow coming out to a small dollar sign. This will represent that the income will be minimal compared to what you have been accustomed and certainly will not be enough to pay for a country club membership or a vacation in Europe. But it will provide some basic needs and may complement your other income sources.

The second source of income is going to come from what is referred to as qualified money. You may be familiar with this as a 401(k) plan or an IRA. Your qualified money box will also yield a stream of income, which will probably be larger than Social Security. Let's draw a slightly bigger box and put in the words 'qualified money,' with an arrow coming out to a medium-size dollar sign.

The third and final source of funds has the propensity to yield the largest amount of monthly income you will receive. Let's draw a larger box with an arrow coming out to a large dollar sign, and in this box let's write (you better pay attention because this is a highly technical term ... ready?): 'Your Own Stuff.'

Your own stuff has the greatest chance of yielding the largest amount of income. But let me ask you:

Who watches to see whether the efficiency of your own stuff meets the current market standard?

Who does that? Does your attorney call and ask you to come in and review the efficiency

Social
Security → $

Qualified
Money → $

Your Own
Stuff → $

of your own stuff? Does your CPA do that?
Who does that?

You see, I think you have a choice. Someday, you
can choose to sit in the Adirondack chairs [point
to the picture on the magazine cover and evoke
some emotion] and enjoy the type of retirement
you always dreamed, or you may choose to be the
next centerfold for *Money Magazine*—maybe the
next substitute for Bill and Barbara Bixler. [At
this point, show the cover of *Money Magazine*
again.] Your choice will depend a lot on whether
you are watching your own stuff and keeping up
with current market standards.

Let me emphasize that …

> **I work with my clients to make sure that
> the efficiency of 'their own stuff' meets
> the current market standard**

… and my ultimate objective is to place you in
those Adirondack chairs.

So, my work centers on identifying enhancements
to your current financial situation and getting you
closer to meeting your personal future dreams.
So tell me: Should we proceed? If so, I would
like to begin asking a few initial questions to get
your opinion on a few financial issues? Would
that be OK?"

EXAMPLE 2
Spouse's Income Need (Life Insurance)

Have you ever wondered how to focus a prospect on the need for insurance while making them emotionally feel the severity of the problem, before moving into a product presentation?

Here is a simple way to dramatically sell the need, allowing you to determine whether you have a prospect who is concerned about the lack of protection for a family or loved one. This example uses the "Rule of 73."

The Rule of 73 is a monetary formula for determining the approximate amount of monthly income generated if you can attain a 7.35% rate of return on a lump sum of money. It is easy to demonstrate and easy to calculate.

The Rule of 73 works by taking any lump sum of money, crossing off the last four digits, and multiplying the number by 60. The result is the amount of monthly income this lump sum of money will yield. Take a look at the worksheet and let's role play.

"Mr. Prospect, have you ever considered whether your insurance meets the current market standard for providing income replacement to your family in the event of your death? Let me walk you through a really quick calculation, and then I would like to get your opinion.

I believe that you stated your income at around $7,000 per month. *$7,000*

Tell me how much insurance you own, including group and individual: *$250,000*

Survivor-Income Calculator

Does your insurance meet the current market standard for providing income and security for your family/spouse in the event of your death? Work through the following hypothetical calculation for a "bread winner" who dies.

Current Monthly Income:	$7,000
Current Insurance (add group and individual policies):	$250,000
Cross off the last 4 numbers of the insurance and place new number here:	25
Multiply the above number by 2 (Daily income provided):	50 *
Multiply the above number by 30 (monthly income provided – before tax):	$1,500 **
Is this the income result you wanted for your family/spouse in the event of your death?	Yes _____ No _____

Note: Calculation does not deduct from insurance proceeds your consumer debt, mortgage payoff, children's college needs, or last medical and funeral expenses. Approximate your liabilities, add those items here $_____ and then recalculate what could be derived from the remaining balance of insurance for income replacement.

When a spouse dies, life insurance is often the most significant source of money from which the family/spouse can make up for the loss in monthly income.

*Income calculation worksheets are available in packs of 50. See the order form at the back of this book.

Cross off the last four numbers of the insurance and put the result here: **25**

Multiply the above number by 2. This is your daily income: **$50**

Multiply the above number by 30. This is your monthly income: **$1,500**

That is the amount of replacement income your spouse would have in the event he or she could invest 100% of your insurance proceeds in an account that yielded a 7.35% return on investment—$1,500 per month.

Mr. Prospect, is this the income result you wanted? Your family just lost $7,000 per month [circle it] and in return is being provided with $1,500 per month [draw an arrow from $7,000 to $1,500]. That is approximately $50 per day [write it and pause] ... and it is still taxable [write it and pause]! Could your family pay their bills with that amount of reduction in income?

Why do you have such little coverage? Did you plan this result or were you just unaware?"

Be quiet. Let the prospect respond. The question is critical, and the answer is of utmost importance.

You don't have a prospect until your prospect verbally admits to having a need.

EXAMPLE 3

Spouse's Income Need
with Mortgage Debt Payoff

Role-play example #3. This demonstrates the
monthly income that's left to live on when a
portion of the insurance proceeds is used to pay
off mortgage or consumer debt. Look at the
worksheet and then follow the script.

Survivor-Income Calculator

Does your insurance meet the current market standard for providing income
and security for your family/spouse in the event of your death? Work through
the following hypothetical calculation for a "bread winner" who dies.

Current Monthly Income: _____

Current Insurance (add group and individual policies): _____

Cross off the last 4 numbers of the insurance
and place new number here: _____

Multiply the above number by 2
(Daily income provided): _____ *

Multiply the above number by 30
(monthly income provided – before tax): _____ **

Is this the income result you wanted for your
family/spouse in the event of your death?   Yes ____ No ____

Note: Calculation does not deduct from insurance proceeds your
consumer debt, mortgage payoff, children's college needs, or last
medical and funeral expenses. Approximate your liabilities, add
those items here $_____ and then recalculate what
could be derived from the remaining balance of insurance for
income replacement.

When a spouse dies, life insurance is often the most significant
source of money from which the family/spouse can make up for the
loss in monthly income.

*Income calculation worksheets are available in packs of 50.
See the order form at the back of this book.

"Mr. Prospect, have you ever considered whether your insurance meets the current market standard for providing income replacement to your family in the event of your death? Let me walk you through a really quick calculation, and then I would like to get your opinion.

I believe you stated your income at about $7,000 per month. **$7,000**

Tell me how much insurance you own, including group and individual: **$250,000**

If you were to die, what debts should be paid off by your spouse?

(Examples might include mortgage, consumer debt, college, funeral) **$180,000**

After paying debts, how much insurance money is left for your spouse? **$70,000**

Cross off the last four numbers of this amount and put the result here: **7**

Multiply the above number by 2. This is your daily income: **$14**

Multiply the above number by 30. This is your monthly income: **$420**

That is the amount of income replacement your spouse would have in the event he or she could invest the remaining amount in an account

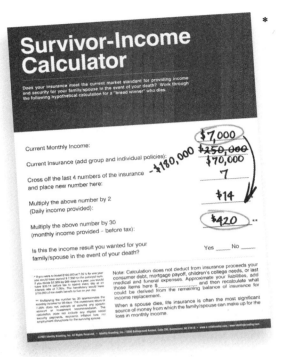

that yielded a 7.35% return on investment — $420 per month.

Mr. Prospect, is this the income result you wanted? Your family just lost $7,000 per month [circle it] and though they paid off some debt, you left them just $420 [draw an arrow from $7,000 to $420 and circle it] for monthly expenses. That is approximately $14 per day ... and it is still taxable!"

(Pause. Then, with conviction and confidence, ask the following.) "Could your family pay their bills with that amount — $420?

*Income calculation worksheets are available in packs of 50. See the order form at the back of this book.

Why do you have such little coverage? Did you plan this result or were you just unaware?"

You may ask what to do if the prospect points out that you did not include Social Security. Simply respond that neither did you include the effects of inflation nor did you provide a cushion fund for unexpected expenses that will arise during their lifetime, such as a new home furnace ($6,000), a new roof, college assistance with the children, a medical crisis, transportation needs, etc.

The point is that many sales are lost because sales people spend too much time on technical issues and lengthy explanations about their products or services before getting a verbal acknowledgment that the prospect feels the pain of the problem.

Though the Rule of 73 formula is simple, you will be amazed at how close it will compare to a computerized, 40-page proposal. Use this formula while having lunch with a prospect, during a fact-finding interview to evaluate if they are open to discuss additional insurance, or as a validation summary after going through a lengthier proposal.

Learn the Rule of 73 formula. It will result in sales that you otherwise would have lost.

EXAMPLE 4
The LTC Need

Have you ever wondered how to quickly determine if a prospect will be receptive to considering Long-Term Care insurance? Here is a simple way to quickly find out if the opportunity exists for such a discussion. Look at the worksheet and then follow the script.

Long-Term Care Calculator

Will your current or projected assets provide the income security you and your spouse may need for assisted living expenses during your retirement years? Work through the following hypothetical calculation and YOU DECIDE.

Estimated qualified money account balance (i.e. 401k, IRA, etc.): _____

Estimate other savings monies that could be used for income: _____

Add together qualified money and savings: _____

Cross off the last 4 numbers above and place new number here: _____

Multiply the above number by 2
(daily income provided): _____

Multiply the above number by 30
(monthly savings income provided – before tax): _____ (1)**

Estimate monthly Social Security income (i.e. $1,800.00): _____ (2)

Add together savings income (1) and Social Security income (2): _____ (a)

What's your estimated monthly
long-term care cost (i.e. $4000 month): _____ (b)

Subtract (b) from (a) to determine the remaining
monthly income for the healthy spouse: _____

Is the remaining income for your spouse adequate? Yes ___ No ___

Should you consider Long-Term Care Insurance? Yes ___ No ___

*Income calculation worksheets are available in packs of 50. See the order form at the back of this book.

"Mr. Prospect, have you looked at the projected cost and chances of either you or your spouse needing long-term care during your retirement years? [Show some statistics.] Have you considered whether you would pay for assisted-living needs from your personal assets or whether insuring against the potential expense would be a better alternative? Let me give you an example:

Let's assume that your future retirement money and cash savings will be worth: **$1,000,000**

Cross off the last four numbers of this amount and put the result here: **100**

Multiply the above number by 60: **6,000***

*This is the amount of monthly income your assets would yield if they were invested and attained a 7.35% return on investment.

What is your estimation of monthly assisted-living costs? **5,000**

Subtract the above estimated cost from your monthly income: **$6,000-$5,000=$1,000**

The **$1,000** is the income left for your spouse or yourself to live on if one of you needs to be placed in an assisted-living facility and the other still needs income for continued living expenses.

Is this amount of income adequate for the person left behind or should you consider long-term care insurance?"

(Be quiet and let the prospect answer. You don't have a prospect until he or she verbally admits to having a need.)

*

Long-Term Care Calculator

Will your current or projected assets provide the income security you and your spouse may need for assisted living expenses during your retirement years? Work through the following hypothetical calculation and YOU DECIDE:

Estimated qualified money account balance (i.e. 401k, IRA, etc.): _____

Estimate other savings monies that could be used for income: **$1,000,000**

Add together qualified money and savings: **100**

Cross off the last 4 numbers above and place new number here: _____ *

Multiply the above number by 2
(daily income provided): _____

Multiply the above number by 30
(monthly savings income provided – before tax): **6,000** (1)**

Estimate monthly Social Security income (i.e. $1,800.00): _____ (2)

Add together savings income (1) and Social Security income (2): _____ (a)

What's your estimated monthly **5,000** (b)
long-term care cost (i.e. $4000 month):

Subtract (b) from (a) to determine the remaining **$1,000**
monthly income for the healthy spouse:

Is the remaining income for your spouse adequate? Yes ____ No ____

Should you consider Long-Term Care Insurance? Yes ____ No ____

*Income calculation worksheets are available in packs of 50.
See the order form at the back of this book.

In summary, whether you are selling investments, insurance, long-term care or any other financial services product, if you don't have a simple way to awfulize the problem that you are trying to solve, your sales success is going to be less than you deserve.

Sell the problem, and any deficiency in the rest of your selling steps is almost forgivable. Selling the problem is where the sale is made!

IT'S YOUR TURN

Write key phrases that you could use to awfulize the financial crisis where you most often focus the majority of your work. Create phrases and sentences that *sell the pain of the problem*.

CHAPTER 7

Step Three:
Invalidate Other Alternatives

This step should encompass 5% of your first meeting.

Eliminate other alternative solutions (without bashing another company) by briefly mentioning how other solutions aren't as effective. For instance, if you're selling financial planning, it is prudent to mention how some people attempt a do-it-yourself approach and then fall short of their financial objectives when it may be too late to take corrective action. Here are some additional examples.

HERE IS THE "HOW-TO"
EXAMPLE 1
Eliminate Other Advisors

After your prospect has bought the problem (but there are competitors who could also deliver a solution) you can effectively eliminate those providers from consideration.

Not only is this an easy step, but it will heighten the prospect's perception of your authority and expertise. It may be as subtle as the following statement:

"Mr. Prospect, who else does this kind of comprehensive work? Does your CPA call and suggest that you make an appointment to discuss whether your assets are meeting the current market standard? Or does your CPA just do a good job on taxes?

Does you attorney call and suggest that you stop by and discuss whether your financial strategy or your retirement strategy is coordinated to take advantage of new tax law changes? Or does he or she just do legal work?

Does your banker do more than just act as a banker—providing a place to save money and get loans?

Does your stockbroker coordinate your financial strategies, or just provide you with occasional good stock picks?

Does your insurance person just sell insurance — car, home, life — but doesn't call and suggest that you frequently get together to look at how your financial strategy is currently meeting the current market standards?

I hope you have the best there is to offer with your selection of a CPA, attorney, banker and stockbroker ... but my focus is one of coordination and overall strategic considerations.

It's about identifying enhancements that may make your overall financial strategies more effective. As we progress, I think you will see the significant value I provide to my clients and why I believe that I am unique within my field."

"Does your stockbroker coordinate your financial strategies, or just provide you with occasional good stock picks?"

EXAMPLE 2
Kill the Do-It-Yourself Argument

"Mr. Prospect, one of the biggest mistakes I encounter — and I encounter this often — is people taking a do-it-yourself approach.

I often find people who have a will, some insurance, some investments, a real estate investment, and maybe a college trust for their children. But they were all put together at separate times, under different circumstances and without any coordination to maximize their effectiveness.

Many times their investments are due to reading *Money Magazine* or getting a 'hot tip' from a friend, and then they wonder years later why the outcome isn't what they had hoped. Do you know people like that?

That's why my work considers all components and attempts to make them work together instead of as separate entities. That's what makes my work unique, as compared to the typical approach. It's a totally coordinated approach."

IT'S YOUR TURN

Write a statement that invalidates alternative strategies that could stall the client moving forward with your next meeting.

CHAPTER 8

Step Four:
Statement of Hope

This step should encompass 5% of your first meeting.

> **Assure the potential client that others who took your advice have been well satisfied with the results.**

It's that simple! It is no different from a sales clerk telling you how happy you are going to be with your purchase. This step isn't just important in retail sales. It is a very reassuring statement and it builds trust.

HERE IS THE "HOW-TO"

> **Words of assurance are always welcomed and comforting to the prospect.**

This is an easy step. Don't overlook it.

EXAMPLE 1
Keeping My Strategies Up-to-Date

"I know that dealing with financial issues can sometimes seem about as exciting as having a root canal, but my clients tell me the end result is well worth the effort. Others tell me that, without my work, many of their strategies would be out-of-date and less effective than they had planned. I believe your experience will be the same. It will be time well spent and the results will help improve the effectiveness of your overall approach to financial issues."

EXAMPLE 2
Staying on Top of Financial Issues

"I know that financial issues aren't always the most exciting items to deal with. It's not like you want to run to the neighbors and invite them over to celebrate your excitement about dealing with items like death, disability and retirement issues. But my clients always tell me how appreciative they are when we complete the process and they feel confident that someone is truly staying on top of their financial issues on a comprehensive basis. They like the fact that someone is paying attention to keeping them up-to-date. I think you will feel the same and I think you will find that we help improve the effectiveness of your strategies."

IT'S YOUR TURN

Write a compelling benefit statement (four or five sentences) that comforts and assures the prospect about the value of your work.

"It's not like you want to run to the neighbors and invite them over to celebrate your excitement about dealing with items like death, disability and retirement issues."

CHAPTER 9

Step Five:
Summarize the Pain, Loss,
& Unwanted Consequences

This step should encompass 10% of your first meeting.

This is a short summary statement before recommending your next step, whether it's a future meeting or permission to begin filling out an application.

When you are in the selling meeting and have been reviewing the product or a recommended solution, or if you are closing your first introductory meeting — *before* asking for an action step, such as the next appointment or permission to begin the application process, don't skip this step!

Make a summary statement that brings the pain, loss and unwanted consequences back into focus.

The greatest chance of getting a sale or an agreement to another meeting is to re-awfulize the pain of the problem.

Do it once again and watch your sales and appointment ratios soar.

HERE IS THE "HOW-TO"

EXAMPLE 1
Before Recommending Additional Insurance or a Second Appointment

"Mr. Prospect, we have spent a lot of time talking about solutions and next steps, but before we proceed any further, I want to focus us back on what we both concluded should be resolved.

As you remember, if we don't resolve the insurance issue, the day may come when your family finds themselves in a horrendous situation.

Let me give you an example by turning the tables for a minute. I want you to imagine a scenario in which your employer fires you and says you will never again have a working income. Would it be difficult for you and your family to survive financially? Even if your spouse worked, would your total loss of income affect your family's lifestyle? Would your children be able to attend college? Would vacations be eliminated? Would eating out or taking an extended weekend trip to the mountains or beach be impossible due to financial hardship?

"As you remember, if we don't resolve the insurance issue, the day may come when your family finds themselves in a horrendous situation."

> **Even if you could pay off the mortgage, would the loss of income require a tremendous amount of sacrifice on everyone's part to make things work?**

That will be your family's situation if we don't resolve the issue of having adequate insurance. The effect on your family, and your children, may last their lifetime. With that in mind, here is what I would suggest...."

EXAMPLE 2
Before Recommending LTC

"Mr. and Mrs. Prospect, we have spent a lot of time talking about solutions and next steps. But before we proceed any further, I want to focus back on the primary issue of long-term care risk.

> **As you remember, if we ignore this issue, the day may come when your financial assets will not be adequate to pay for the unexpected assisted-living expenses for one spouse while the other spouse struggles to survive with adequate income.**

If that were the situation, you would be left with two horrible alternatives: (1) Ignore the needs of the spouse who needs assisted living, causing

him or her to suffer, or (2) take care of the person who needs assisted living while the other spouse tries to get by on the leftover income, which may cause a horrible hardship. Those are two bad choices and neither has to occur when you insure against the loss and hardship. With that in mind, what I would suggest is…."

EXAMPLE 3
Before Suggesting a Second Interview or a Closing Interview

"Mr. Prospect, we have spent a lot of time talking about solutions and how I work with my clients. But before suggesting the next step, I want to focus us back on what I consider are the real issues and why we should proceed.

> **Though my work concentrates on helping clients find enhancements to their financial strategies, the real objective is to avoid the pain that could be caused when they don't take these recommended actions.**

You and I both know couples who reach retirement and think they are in pretty good shape, only to find out later that their planning just didn't meet all of their objectives.

I think we both agree that …

money isn't everything, but when you retire, money has a lot to do with how interesting and satisfying our lives will be during our golden years.

Being able to travel, help our children and grand-children financially, maybe take them on a trip occasionally, these are the types of things that most of my clients want to maximize to the fullest. But if you don't adequately keep up with changing market conditions, tax laws and financial strategies, you may live your final years with regret, knowing that you could have done so much better.

You know, retirement isn't a second-chance sport. We get one shot at it.

And my objective is to help my clients find the enhancements that make the most of those years.

With that in mind, what I would suggest is ...."

IT'S YOUR TURN

Write a summary statement that briefly re-awfulizes the typical problem you sell. This is your last chance to bring the prospect back to the emotional issue of your proposal or to establish a compelling reason to meet with you again.

"As you remember, if we ignore this issue, the day may come when your financial assets will not be adequate..."

CHAPTER 10
Step Six:
Request Specific Action
with a Benefit Statement

This step should encompass 5% of your first meeting.

Many advisors are very skilled at engaging the prospect in first interview conversations or assembling and presenting a proposal. But they fail to ask a closing question that mandates a yes or no response on behalf of the prospect. The result is an opening interview that goes nowhere or a presentation close that never materializes.

Don't meekly ask, "What do you think?"

Don't make a statement such as, "This seems to work really well in meeting your goals," while letting the conversation then drop off into silence.

Don't keep talking about one extra item because you're afraid to ask a closing question.

Be brave, direct and ask a yes or no question for your next action step. Now ... be quiet and let them answer.

The prospect is not going to initiate a request to fill out an application or suggest that you check your schedule to see when you can come back and meet for a fact-finding interview. It is your job to ask a specific yes or no closing question to a specific action and then let the person answer! If you want to increase your sales, tell the prospect specifically what you want and wait for a response! Wait, wait, and wait some more! Let them answer. It will make you look professional and confident.

> **To maximize your success, ask the prospect for a specific yes or no to a well-defined action question after you have made a brief benefit statement. Now ... keep quiet and wait for an answer.**

There are two exceptions to a yes or no question:

1. If your action step is to set another meeting, ask for a choice of dates and times, such as "Can we meet again either next Tuesday at 2 p.m. or Wednesday at 3 p.m.?"

2. If during a sales presentation you make an implied statement of acceptance to your proposal and then proceed directly into an application by asking an application question. See examples on following pages.

HERE IS THE "HOW-TO"

EXAMPLE 1

If this is a large case, or the prospect seems to want a lot of control, request a meeting with a "proposal draft" to help diffuse any objection.

"I am going to need about a week to assemble a preliminary draft on some potential enhancements to your current strategy that I think may provide you with more security at retirement and allow you to feel more assured about your retirement objectives. Since it will be a working draft, my objective during this meeting will be to get your ideas on what you like and what we should change in order to best meet your specific goals. Would it be more convenient for you to meet to do this draft review on Tuesday at 2 p.m. or would Wednesday at 3 p.m. be better for you?"

EXAMPLE 2

Make an implied statement of mutual acceptance and begin the application.

"It appears to me that this solution does a great job in meeting your objectives — providing more security for you, your spouse and your children. Let me get your Social Security number. We will need it to begin the underwriting review on the protection amount, as well as for the application process. What is your Social Security number?"

(Note: Starting a sales application usually proceeds best if you begin with a very simple, non-threatening question. It is not necessary to start the application process with the first question on the application, which was probably designed by a data entry person and not someone whose specialty is human behavior. Start your application with a non-threatening question—one that doesn't raise an objection about price or product.)

EXAMPLE 3

After the initial (first) interview, request a fact-finding meeting by adding an effective benefit statement.

"I would like to get together again with you. A second meeting would allow me adequate time to gather some additional information, which would guide me in making the best enhancement suggestions. It would also allow you to offer your opinion and guide the discussion on how we should mold any recommendations to help maximize your objectives. I believe that our joint effort would result in increasing the financial results for your retirement years, as well as provide added security for your family.

Would next Tuesday at 3 p.m. be a good time for our next meeting?"

IT'S YOUR TURN

Write a statement that describes the action you want from your prospect. If you have difficulty getting a second appointment, focus on a benefit statement that will convince the prospect to meet with you again. Make sure you include a benefit statement or it won't be effective.

CHAPTER **11**

Summary

I hope you have enjoyed this brief book and that you have learned the six steps of problem communication. If you will now use them, they will stimulate greater desirable action with your prospects. In other words, *you will sell more*!

Remember, today's prospect is more skeptical, more informed and wiser to the approaches of the financial advisor than in years past. That doesn't mean people won't grant an occasional appointment. All of us experience times in our lives (a financial disaster, the death of a family member or close friend) that make us receptive to discussing insurance or financial issues.

But if you want to be thoughtfully strategic in getting consistently better results, learn to communicate problems… *NOT SOLUTIONS*.

The difference can be profound.

In summary, here are the six steps that you need to incorporate into your daily habit of communication. If you want to maximize your results, take the time to review these steps every time you miss a sale. Chances are … you missed a step.

Step 1. State the Problem (5%)

Step 3. Invalidate Other Alternatives (5%)

Step 4. Make a Statement of Hope (5%)

Step 5. Summarize the Pain, Loss
and Unwanted Consequences (10%)

Step 6. Request Specific Action
with a Benefit Statement (5%)

Though there are six steps, if I could plant *one item* in your mind, it would be Step 2: *awfulize the problem*!

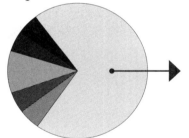

AWFULIZE
THE PROBLEM

Remember, don't just identify a general problem and then proceed into a conversation about how you work. Identify the pain, the loss and the unwanted consequences of the prospect's current course of action and drive it home until it hurts.

Awfulize the problem!

Accentuate the emotional pain of the problem.

Ask the client how he or she feels about the problem.

Listen for the prospect to verbally admit to having a problem.

Ask the prospect to express how the problem may affect him or her.

And then, if you don't hear the prospect repeat back the potential pain of the current financial situation ... leave. You don't have a prospect.

When a prospect won't verbalize the potential pain, go find someone else to talk to. You will be happier, and you will make more money.

Postlude

What do you sell?

Problems or solutions?

That question was posted to a large group of Million Dollar Round Table Producers after a one-hour keynote speech, and it caused a thunderous answer to fill the room. "PROBLEMS! WE SELL PROBLEMS!"

They got it!!!

Those were the superstars!

SELL THE PROBLEM.

The prospect will beg for a solution.

About the Author

Robert E. Krumroy

CEO, author of six books and founder of Identity Branding, Inc. and e-Relationship, has been teaching the principles of prospect attraction to financial sales professionals for more than 30 years. His impressive career placed him among the top 100 financial managers in the financial industry. Referred to as The Prospect-Attraction Coach, Robert is a nationally recognized speaker and teacher. The powerful strategy he teaches has dramatically improved sales, prospect access, retention and recruiting for many of the leading financial service companies in the U.S. He lives in Greensboro, NC.

Advisor Toolbox

Competitive products are no longer unique. Advanced support is not a differentiator. Hope is not a strategy.

Take a day to build an attraction strategy, be consistent in implementation, and watch your reputation soar above the norm.

It is the wise business person who dares to open his or her mind to new ways of capturing clients and outperforming the competition.

Allow me to introduce you to a powerful set of programs and tools created by Identity Branding that will give you the inspiration, motivation and skills to be consistently successful.

Survivor-Income Calculator

Does your insurance meet the current market standard for providing income and security for your family/spouse in the event of your death? Work through the following hypothetical calculation for a "bread winner" who dies.

Current Monthly Income: .... _____

Current Insurance: .... _____
(add group and individual policies)

Cross off the last 4 numbers of the insurance
and place new number here: .... _____

Multiply the above number by 2: .... _____ *
(daily income provided)

Multiply the above number by 30: .... _____ **
(monthly income provided — before tax)

Is this the income result you wanted for your
family/spouse in the event of your death? .... Yes _____ No _____

* If you were to invest $100,000 at 7.35% for one year you would have earned $7,350 on the principal sum. If you divide $7,350 by 365 days in a year, you would have $20.14 before tax to spend every day at an interest rate of 7.35%. The beneficiary would have 2/10,000 of the death benefit to live on per day.
** Multiplying the number by 30 approximates the monthly income for 30 days. The investment return of 7.35% does not indicate or assume any specific account or investment recommendation. The calculation does not include any eligible Social Security payments, economic inflation loss, nor employment disruptions for the surviving spouse.

Note: Calculation does not deduct from insurance proceeds your consumer debt, mortgage payoff, children's college needs, or last medical and funeral expenses. Approximate your liabilities, add those items here $_____ and then recalculate what could be derived from the remaining balance of insurance for income replacement.

When a spouse dies, life insurance is often the most significant source of money from which the family/spouse can make up for the loss in monthly income.

Calculator worksheets are available in pads of 50.
See page 89.

Long-Term Care Calculator

Will your current or projected assets provide the income security you and your spouse may need for assisted living expenses during your retirement years? Work through the following hypothetical calculation and *you decide*:

Estimated qualified money account balance
(i.e. 401k, IRA, etc.): .... _____

Estimate other savings monies that
could be used for income: .... _____

Add together qualified money and savings: .... _____

Cross off the last 4 numbers above
and place new number here: .... _____

Multiply the above number by 2: .... _____ *
(daily income provided)

Multiply the above number by 30: .... _____ (1)**
(monthly savings income provided — before tax)

Estimate monthly Social Security income
(i.e. $1,800.00): .... _____ (2)

Add together savings income (1)
and Social Security income (2): .... _____ (a)

What's your estimated monthly
long-term care cost (i.e. $4000 month): .... _____ (b)

Subtract (b) from (a) to determine the remaining
monthly income for the healthy spouse: .... _____

Is the remaining income for
your spouse adequate? .... Yes ____ No ____

Should you consider
Long-Term Care Insurance? .... Yes ____ No ____

---

* If you were to invest $100,000 at 7.35 % for one year you would have earned $ 7,350 on the principal sum. If you divide $7,350 by 365 days in a year, you would have $20.14 before tax to spend every day at an interest rate of 7.35%. The beneficiary would have 2/10,000 of the death benefit to live on per day.
** Multiplying the number by 30 approximates the monthly income for 30 days. The investment return of 7.35% does not indicate or assume any specific account or investment recommendation. The calculation does not include any eligible Social Security payments, economic inflation loss, nor employment disruptions for the surviving spouse.

Please...Make ME a little bit FAMOUS!

A MUST READ!

In this book, Robert offers a cutting-edge approach to creating prospect attraction in today's skeptical marketplace. His first book, Identity Branding—Creating Prospect Attraction, was reprinted four times and is still used in study groups all over America. This new book takes the practical advice even further. It has over 180 pages describing in detail the newest prospect attraction strategies – examples that show sales professionals how to open doors to desirable prospects and make themselves a little bit FAMOUS in their local communities.

Please...Make ME a little Bit FAMOUS! Complete Marketing Kit

Robert Krumroy's acclaimed financial industry book *Please...Make ME a little bit FAMOUS* is now available on CD, with 21 mini-marketing booklets as a bonus. This marketing kit is a must-have if you want to build dominant recognition in your local community. Each of the booklets reveals an awareness strategy used by super achievers to build recognition, surprise, delight and appreciation with prospects and clients. Just choose or adapt the strategy that fits your personality and market. All of the information you need to implement a strategy (including sample letters and order forms) are included here. It's an unbeatable way to learn how to open doors in your market.

The Prospect Relationship Ladder

Old traditional methods of "getting in" don't work - not like they use to; even better phone approaches produce minimal improvements. Today's methods and systems for gaining prospect access are new and must be learned. Helping your prospect climb the Relationship Ladder to the Emotional Safety Rung 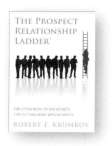 will cause your appointment success to soar...as well as significantly impact your sales! Read this book.

It's NOT About Luck!

Impression management is the new skill for creating prospect attraction and solving your advisor's appointment activity challenge. As a manager, nothing will cause greater appointment and production increases than directing your advisors in building effective prospect-attraction strate-  gies. When done correctly, clients will increase their loyalty and prospects will enthusiastically agree to appointments with your advisors, concluding that they are remarkable and far superior to the competition. Apply this new skill and watch your advisor's activity, production, retention, recruiting and your firm's reputation soar to new heights.

Identity Branding Revisited—Creating Prospect Attraction

FOR FINANCIAL PLANNERS AND INSURANCE AGENTS

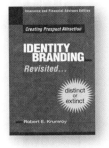

Already in its *fourth printing*, this is the most talked about marketing book in the financial industry. Within 9 months of being released, a *second printing* was required. Over 200 pages that give you the secrets to creating a visible differentiation in the marketplace; a client perception of superior value; a consumer preference for *you*.

Don't miss this powerful book.

Brilliant Strategies and Fatal Blunders

THIS BOOK IS A MUST READ!

Working hard, providing a quality product or being personally determined to "gut it out" until people recognize your expertise and give you their business no longer attains high-level success. High-level success requires critical thinking; building visible market differentiation; and then outclassing the competition. This book identifies the *brilliant* strategies used by professionals, service companies and retail establishments to do just that ... *beat the competition and thrive*. But caution, the *fatal blunders* are practically invisible and almost always terminal. If you want to survive and thrive, read this book.

Marketing Booklets

Every advisor has a "getting in" problem in today's environment. Prospects, even referrals, are hesitant to say "yes" to an appointment request. The bottom line is if you want to solve the "getting in" problem, you must apply a "getting in" solution. Separating *you* from the competition requires differentiation and high-level consistent visibility. Consistent visibility is the hallmark of attraction. Heightening awareness of *you* and your differentiated business reputation is critical for gaining attraction. Frequent visibility is imperative if you expect the majority of your appointment requests to be accepted. Robert Krumroy, President of Identity Branding/e-Relationship, has developed Creating Prospect Approachability Booklets, which provide ideas that produce exceptional results.

Please…Make ME a little bit FAMOUS!
The Prospect Attraction Workshop

- *Increase Sales!*
- *Obtain Welcomed Appointments!*
- *Raise Your Referral Rate!*
- *Develop a 1-Year Personal Branding Plan!*
- *Attain Greater Career Satisfaction!*

In this concise and lively program, we teach you how to create a market attraction strategy that elevates your personal visibility, professional image, confidence and prospect approachability. The workshop is available in either a 2½-hour or five-hour format and includes a 14-page workbook for each participant. The agenda includes:

1 HISTORY

What has changed in the marketplace? It isn't an illusion; it is harder to get in to see prospects than any time in history … and old techniques aren't working. The advisor must learn and engage the six new psychological rules of attraction to achieve high-level success.

2 ENGAGE YOUR TARGETED PROSPECTS

Teaching advisors how to heighten their local market attraction and credibility through uniquely engaging their prospect clusters will build likeability and market separation. These strategies increase advisors' confidence, as well as prospect approachability.

The session ends with each advisor identifying a strategic event(s) that he or she will embrace to build personal local recognition and affection to a specific audience.

3 Character Uniqueness

Identify ways that advisors can tightly bond to their top 20 clients and centers of influence. The result is increased sales and a continuous flow of invaluable referrals throughout the year. Once a strategy is implemented, advisors will improve their positioning, image, differentiation, referral flow and visibility to their top clients and targeted prospects.

4 Staying Connected

Out of sight, out of mind! Getting and staying connected to prospects and clients is the foundation of attraction and creating deep client loyalty. There is no more effective way to open doors, build market separation and establish superior credibility than by delivering consistent "top of mind" touch points. If you want increased appointments and welcomed access to new prospects, learn the secrets to effective connection.

e-relationship™

The number-one e-connection tool in the financial industry!

Consistent connection is one of the mainstays of being a highly successful financial advisor. Our e-Relationship automated email program makes it delightfully easy to keep in touch with every prospect and client in your database. Send holiday e-cards, e-birthday wishes, e-newsletters and more throughout the year. Also choose from 75 prepackaged financial e-briefs. Each message is personalized and sent one at a time — *no multiple-name mailing list is ever seen by your recipients.*

www.e-relationship.com

Agent-Recruiting.com is the recruiting module of e-Relationship.com. The recruiting module is filled with e-Recruiting Storyboards that will attract immediate raise-your-hand responses from potential new and experienced agents. The animated e-recruiting messages not only attract new recruits, but also demonstrate how your company supports unique marketing, which can lead to an easy discussion of how you help agents create a distinctive business image within their community.

www.agent-recruiting.com

Please provide information on:

❑ Prospect Attraction Workshops   ❑ Speaking Engagements

Books:

❑ *Sell the Problem — The Prospect Will Beg For A Solution!*..... $9⁹⁵ _____
❑ *The Prospect Relationship Ladder*.................................. $16⁹⁵ _____
❑ *Please...Make ME a little bit FAMOUS!*...................... $24⁹⁵ _____
❑ *Please...Make ME a little bit FAMOUS! Audio Version* ..... $39⁹⁵ _____
❑ *Identity Branding – Revisited* .... $19⁹⁵ _____
❑ *Brilliant Strategies and Fatal Blunders*........................... $18⁹⁵ _____
❑ *It's NOT About Luck!* (Manager Book) .... $39⁹⁵ _____

Marketing Kit:

❑ *Please...Make ME a little bit FAMOUS!*
Complete Marketing Kit (Includes 21 Idea Booklets)............... $99⁹⁵ _____

Calculation Worksheets

Survivor-Income Calculator (Life Insurance)........ ❑ 1 Pad (50 copies): $12⁹⁵
                                                    ❑ 5 Pads (250 copies): $49⁹⁵

Long-Term Care Calculator .... ❑ 1 Pad (50 copies): $12⁹⁵
                                                    ❑ 5 Pads (250 copies): $49⁹⁵

Total $ _____

Payment Information

Name _____ Phone Number _____

Company _____

Email Address _____

Office Mailing Address _____

City _____ State _____ Zip Code _____

Card Number _____ Expiration Date _____

Signature _____

❑ AMEX ❑ MasterCard ❑ VISA ❑ Discover ❑ Invoice Me

NOTE: Additional S/H charges will apply.

Fax to 336-303-7318